THE CAGE WITHIN

PRISON OF OWN THOUGHTS

Manvi Jain

BlueRose ONE.com
Stories Matter
NewDelhi • London

BLUEROSE PUBLISHERS
India | U.K.

BlueRoseONE.com
Stories Matter
NewDelhi • London

For permissions requests or inquiries regarding this publication, please contact:

BLUEROSE PUBLISHERS
www.BlueRoseONE.com
info@bluerosepublishers.com
+91 8882 898 898
+4407342408967

ISBN: 978-93-7542-873-2

Cover design: Rohit
Typesetting: Namrata Saini

First Edition: January 2026

To the ones who taught me strength without ever saying a word.
To the ones who stood, even in silence.

Acknowledgement

This book is not just mine; it belongs to every silent soul who ever carried a burden no one else could see. To those who battled in silence, who cried behind closed doors, who questioned their worth yet woke up every morning to fight again - this is for you.

I thank the invisible strength within me that refused to let go, even when my mind tried to surrender. I am deeply grateful to the people who shaped my journey; some with love, some with hurt, but all teaching me what I could not have learned otherwise.

And finally, to the reader - you. If even a single page of this book feels like it was written for you, then my silence has found its voice.

For You, Who Feels

We live in a world where cages are not always built with iron; they are built inside our minds. A thousand expectations, rejections, comparisons, and judgments weave invisible bars around us. We may smile, we may work, we may even succeed, but deep inside, our wings remain folded, aching to fly.

The Cage Within: Prison of Own Thoughts is the story of countless hearts. It is about how pain enters quietly, how silence becomes heavy, and how we unknowingly trap ourselves in chains made of fear and guilt. But it is also about breaking those chains.

This book is for those who have ever asked themselves:

- *Why does no one understand me?*
- *Why am I never enough?*
- *Why do my choices never matter?*

If you have ever carried these questions, if you have ever felt like screaming but stayed silent instead; then this book is your reflection.

Every soul carries its own quiet storms, its hidden struggles, and unspoken longings. This book is not a map for the perfect life, nor a prescription to erase pain. It is a companion, a voice that whispers: *You are seen. You are understood. You are not alone.*

I wrote these words for the moments when the world feels too heavy, when every expectation weighs on your chest, and the very air seems hard to breathe. For the times you have smiled through the ache, stayed silent when your heart wanted to speak, and carried burdens that no one else could notice.

Within these pages, you will find stories, reflections, and gentle guidance; not as someone else's solution, but as a mirror to your own journey. To help you recognize the cage that may have quietly formed around your thoughts, your choices, your freedom... and to offer a way to begin opening it, brick by brick.

This book is a reminder that no one else can walk in your shoes, and yet, in reading these words, you are not alone. Your emotions are valid, your struggles are real, and your courage is already within you, waiting to be recognized.

If these pages awaken a whisper of hope, a flicker of understanding, or even a quiet smile for yourself, then the journey of this book has already begun.

Read gently. Reflect deeply. And remember; your heart, your soul, and your truth matter more than anyone else's expectations.

The Voices Behind These Pages

This book was not born in isolation.

It grew quietly, like a tree rooted in shared silence; watered by the tears, whispers, and unspoken truths of many souls. Over the course of months, I spoke with more than a hundred people: some in crowded cafés, some through late-night messages, some in hushed corners where words finally dared to breathe.

They came from different cities, careers, families, and ages. Yet their stories carried the same invisible ache; of trying too hard to be understood, of bending under the weight of expectations, of fighting battles no one else could see. Some called it burnout, others despair, some simply said, "I feel tired of being strong."

These were not interviews with checklists. They were *open doors* into the inner rooms of their lives. Each story; fragile, powerful, unfinished; became a quiet mirror, reflecting the shared wounds we so often believe are ours alone.

I carry their voices between these pages not as statistics, but as a reminder: pain is never isolated, and neither is the will to rise. Every insight in this book is stitched with the threads of these real conversations; honest, raw, and humane.

May their whispers reach you as softly as they reached me.

How to Walk Through This Book

This book is not meant to be read in a hurry.
It is a journey; quiet, unfolding, and deeply human.
Each chapter meets you exactly where you are and carries you gently to where you need to be.

Pain has a story.
Healing has a direction.
And freedom has a rhythm of its own.

This book follows that rhythm.

Part I - The Cage We Do Not See

This part explores the shadows we seldom acknowledge: the first wounds, the inherited expectations, the silent guilt, the invisible cages.
You will walk through:

- how pain first takes shape,
- how love becomes heavy,
- how unspoken expectations bind us,
- and how the mind can imprison itself through fear, self-doubt, and overthinking.

It also introduces the Jain philosophy of *anekantvad* - the truth that no single perspective is complete.
This opens the doorway to compassion: for yourself, for those who hurt you unintentionally, and for the complexity of human lives.

This section is not about blame.
It is about understanding the architecture of your own pain.

Part II - The Unfolding Within

If Part I shows the cage, Part II begins to loosen its bars.
Here, the journey turns inward:

- discovering why no one else can rescue you,
- rebuilding a relationship with yourself,
- accepting reality without surrendering your soul,
- letting go through detachment, forgiveness, and clarity,
- and learning the quiet revolution of choosing peace over people-pleasing.

This part teaches you that healing is not dramatic;
it is subtle, patient, and born from honesty.
It is where you begin to breathe again.

Part III - The Path Beyond the Cage

The final section is a guide; not to tell you how to live, but to help you return home to yourself.
It offers:

- daily rituals,
- reflection journals,
- affirmation practices inspired by Shri Praman Sagar Ji Maharaj,
- the real voices of people who trusted their pain with you,
- 30 days of gentle healing prompts,

- and a closing prose that honors your journey.

These tools are meant to be practiced slowly,
so the healing can settle not just in your mind,
but in your breath, habits, and inner voice.

Your Journey, Page by Page

If you read with openness,
Part I will make you feel understood,
Part II will help you transform,
and Part III will accompany you
as you learn to live freely again;
not in rebellion,
but in self-respect.
This book holds your hand from darkness to clarity,
from fear to acceptance,
from survival to truth,
and finally;
to the quiet joy of belonging to yourself.

The Death That Breathes

The real death is not when the body stops breathing.
It is when something inside you stops wanting to breathe.
When your laughter becomes practiced,
your eyes learn to hide more than they reveal,
and your silence becomes the only language that feels safe.
The world mourns the death that ends a heartbeat,
but no one notices the ones that die quietly while still alive,
the dreams that were never spoken,
the truths that were never heard,
the love that was always offered, never returned.
Sometimes death comes dressed as routine;
as a job that kills the spirit one email at a time,
as a home that echoes with unspoken words,
as a smile that survives out of habit.
And yet, there is something sacred even in this dying;
because the moment we recognize what has withered within,
the possibility of rebirth begins.
The same pain that once destroyed us
can become the fire that rebuilds us.
Perhaps this is what life truly is;
not a battle to avoid death,
but a journey to keep our inner flame alive
in a world that keeps trying to blow it out.

Contents

What is Pain?

When a soul arrives in this world, it arrives untouched. Pure. Unburdened. No history clings to it, no shadows follow it, no debts or promises hold it down. It is like an empty sky; limitless, weightless, waiting to be filled with colors.

But the moment that soul enters a body, a journey begins. A child is born not by choice, not with consent, not with a list of desires. The child arrives with empty hands; no love, no sorrow, no expectation. Just breath. Just life.

And then, life begins its gentle shaping. The child, like soft clay, learns from the world around; smiling when someone smiles back, crying when comfort does not arrive, feeling joy in praise, shrinking in correction. Each moment becomes a quiet lesson, forming the child's sense of self. In this way, the soul's boundless freedom slowly takes shape within the patterns of the world it grows into.

What we call "growing up" is often just the art of learning what others want us to learn. Rarely do we see the world as an open field of play, of wonder. Instead, we are taught what is safe, what is right, what is expected.

But here lies the root of pain: our subconscious was meant to remain free, like the soul itself. It was designed to explore, to choose, to discover who we are. Instead, it is trained and fed by external voices; sometimes loving, sometimes harsh, always demanding. Slowly, a quiet war begins inside us. Who we are collides with who we are told to be.

This contradiction, this inner chaos; that is where pain is born. Not in the body, not in the events of life, but in the silent space between our true self and the self we are forced to carry.

It is said that a soul is freed from the cycle of birth and death only when it is released from all karmic bonds. Perhaps the same is true of living. We find peace only when we free ourselves from borrowed expectations and begin to live by choice - our choice. Only then can we leave this world satisfied, wings open, sky endless, soul unchained.

"Pain is born when the free soul forgets its own voice beneath the many voices that guide it. To find peace, we do not have to fight the world; we only have to remember ourselves."

Pain is not a wound, it is the echo of what mattered.
It is the proof that something once lived deeply inside us;
a hope, a bond, a promise we believed was unbreakable.
It is the mirror that shows us our most fragile truths,
not to punish, but to remind us we can feel.
Pain is love with nowhere left to go.
It is the language the soul speaks
when the world has forgotten how to listen.

Part I
The Cage We Do Not See

Chapter-1
When Pain Finds a Home

Pain is born when the love we trust the most suddenly feels distant, and the walls we believed safe reveal their cracks.

The Unheard Conversations

"I always thought home was safety, until I realized every choice I made was quietly weighed, and I was always found lacking."

– mid-30s professional

"The people I loved the most became the ones I feared speaking to; their silence was heavier than any punishment."

– young adult, struggling with family expectations

"It wasn't what they said that broke me, but the invisible line I had crossed; the moment I existed for myself, not their dreams."

– early 20s, recent graduate

There is a place we call home,
Where laughter echoes and warmth feels endless.
Yet even in this shelter, shadows settle softly,
And words, gentle or harsh, leave marks unseen.
A child learns here what the heart can carry,
What it can hope for, and what it cannot hold.
The world outside waits patiently,
But the first lessons come from the walls around us.

The First Stirrings of Pain

Pain often arrives not as a sudden blow, but as a quiet, almost imperceptible ripple in the mind of a child. It begins in the moments when what we feel, what we wish to express, is not fully acknowledged; not out of malice, but because the world around us is structured differently. Parenting, guidance, and care are often one-way streets: the lessons are delivered, the boundaries are set, the rules are clear; but the inner voice of the child is rarely invited into the conversation.

Imagine a small heart learning to speak, to share, to hope. And each time it stretches, it meets silence, a gentle redirect, or a sigh of disapproval. Nothing violent, nothing dramatic; but enough for a subtle question to grow in the mind: *Do my feelings matter? Am I enough just as I am?*

This is the point where curiosity begins to coexist with hesitation, where innocence begins to feel the weight of expectation. The child learns early that approval often comes not for authenticity, but for alignment: alignment with ideals, with dreams, with comfort zones carefully curated by others. The more this continues, the more a soft inner caution develops; a quiet restraint that teaches a child to measure, to adjust, to hold back.

Over time, these small lessons accumulate. They shape confidence in ways invisible yet profound. A child who feels heard, even occasionally, carries the courage to experiment, to express, to make choices boldly. A child who feels consistently overlooked begins to measure their worth against others' standards, learning early that self-expression carries risk. This subtle difference; the difference between being truly seen and simply being guided; creates the foundation for personality, for self-belief, for the courage to navigate life.

And here, pain first finds a subtle home: not as rebellion, not as hurt inflicted by others, but as a quiet tension between what the heart knows it feels and what the world acknowledges. It is the first hint that life is not only about survival or guidance, but also about the delicate art of finding one's own voice amidst the chorus of expectations.

Learning Through Contradictions

Life's guidance is never uniform. Some lessons nurture, others restrict, and some do both simultaneously. This is where confusion quietly begins. The child is encouraged to be thoughtful, careful, and attentive to the needs of others, yet the mind is simultaneously learning that the self has desires of its own.

The subconscious, by design, is meant to roam freely. It thrives on discovery, exploration, and the gentle unfolding of one's inner truth. When external voices- whether from teachers, peers, or those closest; provide direction that subtly contradicts these instincts, a quiet inner conflict emerges. Who am I? Whose voice am I listening to? Where do my own choices begin?

These are questions without immediate answers. And in that uncertainty, the first seeds of pain are sown. They do not hurt as sharply as a wound, but they linger like a low hum, a quiet weight pressing softly yet persistently against the heart.

It is a delicate tension: the love and guidance that have helped shape a child's world are intertwined with the subtle realization that not all directions, not all expectations, align perfectly with the soul's inner compass.

The Weight of Awareness

Gradually, awareness grows. The child begins to notice patterns: the weight of unspoken rules, the soft but persistent shaping of choices, the gentle steering of attention and behavior. Nothing here is intended as harm, and yet the realization of constraint is unavoidable. The bubble of unbounded freedom that once existed feels smaller, reshaped by circumstance and care.

This recognition brings its own form of grief. It is the first sense of disappointment; not in others, but in the discrepancy between life as imagined and life as experienced. It is the first moment when the world appears not entirely safe, not entirely predictable, not entirely one's own.

And in this fragile space, a quiet resilience begins to form. The child learns patience, careful observation, and emotional attunement. They learn to navigate the delicate balance between inner desire and outer reality. They learn, often without words, that pain is not always a call to fight;

it can be a guide, a teacher, a quiet companion, helping to illuminate the boundaries between self and world.

Reflection on Early Pain

Even as one grows, the echoes of these early experiences remain. The awareness that life is layered, that love and expectation are intertwined, that freedom is discovered gradually; these truths linger quietly in the mind. Pain, in this sense, is not a punishment. It is the gentle opening of consciousness, the soft awakening to the fact that life is neither entirely under control nor entirely outside it.

The most profound lessons of childhood are rarely taught with speeches or instructions; they arrive as feelings, as subtle realizations, as small moments of confusion and wonder. And when these moments accumulate, they create a space where the soul begins to recognize itself; not just in reflection of the world around, but in quiet observation of its own heartbeat.

Even now, when one writes, speaks, or reflects, there is often a cautious awareness of perception: how will others understand this? Will they see the intention, the reflection, the inner journey? Yet the act of observation, of gentle acknowledgment, is itself a step toward freedom.

Pain, when it first finds a home, is not meant to break a soul. It is meant to awaken it. It is the first teacher, showing that the life we are given is complex, layered, and deeply worth exploring.

"Pain is not a shadow cast by others, nor a judgment upon us. It is the quiet invitation to meet ourselves, to notice our own wings waiting beneath the weight, and to learn that freedom begins in gentle awareness."

Shaped by the Silences Around Us

A child does not learn trust from words; it learns it from the quiet spaces between them.
Before we learn the language of the world, we learn the language of presence; the warmth of a look, the calm of a hand that does not let go, the assurance that someone will be there when the shadows grow longer.
The earliest surroundings of a child are not just walls and windows, they are entire universes.
They shape what the child will believe about love, safety, and worth. A voice raised in anger, a hurried step, a distracted glance; these become invisible brushstrokes, painting the first sketches of a mind. And what begins as momentary silences slowly grows into the architecture of a person's inner world.

Many children grow up in homes that carry both love and struggle in the same breath. Parents, fighting their own battles, often love deeply but show it through duty, not presence. The child understands more than anyone realizes. It watches the mother rush between responsibilities, the father hustling against life's constant demands, and quietly learns: "My feelings can wait. My needs are not urgent."

When emotional space shrinks, childhood adapts. A little boy or girl begins to step back, to become quieter, to not demand what they know cannot be given. The longing to play outside turns into the responsibility of helping at home. The excitement of school achievements fades into the fear of adding "more work" to an already burdened parent. Love is never doubted, but its language changes; it becomes a silence that teaches compliance, not expression.

Years pass. Childhood ends. But what is learned in silence does not leave with age. The grown-up still carries the small child inside; the one who learned not to ask for too much, who measured their worth by how little space they could take. And when adulthood brings its own storms, the buried ache finds new ways to surface. A late-night argument. A job rejection. A careless word. Each moment awakens the echoes of a childhood that whispered, "Be grateful, not demanding. Be strong, not seen."

What often appears as depression in the present is not born in a single day. It is layered. It grows in the spaces where love existed but presence did not. Where parents did their best, but survival overshadowed softness. Where emotions were acknowledged only when they became unbearable.

And this is where the paradox lies; those who gave their everything often could not give what was needed the most: emotional safety. Not because they did not love, but because they, too, were shaped by their own silent storms.

As adults, we return to these foundations not to blame, but to understand. Because pain is not only what happened to

us; it is also what remained unspoken.
And until we learn to name those silences, they continue to speak for us.

Chapter – 2
The Silent Weight of Expectations

The silent weight of expectations does not shout; it whispers. It whispers in your choices, in your silences, in your restless nights. It does not always kill, but it steals color from life, one shade at a time.

The Unheard Conversations

"Every decision felt like a crime, even the ones I knew were right for me. I lived as if I owed the world an apology."

– *28-year-old, corporate employee*

"I begged for patience, for understanding; and instead, I received instructions, comparisons, and silent judgment."

– *31-year-old woman*

"I began to measure my worth in the reflection of other people's satisfaction, forgetting my own face in the mirror."

– *mid-20s, struggling with career and relationships*

Expectations do not arrive with thunder,
they slip quietly into our veins.
Dreams not our own begin to take root,
and we wear them as if they were skin.
Every nod of approval feels like love,
every refusal, a wound too deep to name.
And somewhere between duty and desire,
the soul begins to forget its own language.

Two Paths of Response

Life often divides people into two unseen categories.

The first kind are the straightforward ones. They hear the voices of others, but they walk their own road. They may face anger, arguments, even rejection; but they do not bend easily under the weight of expectation. Their families might rage, might scold, but once the storm passes, life resumes. No hearts are broken, only tempers flared. This path, though not easy, is less consuming; for anger can be endured, but emotional entanglement lingers much longer.

The second kind of journey, however, is far heavier. This is where every expectation is tied to love, where every choice becomes an emotional battlefield. Here, pain is not in raised voices, but in lowered ones. Not in loud rejection, but in the silent burden of guilt. Every decision feel like a wound, because it is never only about you; it becomes about your family's pride, their dreams, their fears of society's whisper.

When Love Learns to Fear

In most of the homes, the family itself is not the enemy. In fact, they often carry immense love. But love, when tangled with fear, becomes suffocating. Parents wish to protect their child; but not only from failure, also from the imagined judgment of neighbors, relatives, the so-called society that no one truly owns.

It is here the generational gap cuts the deepest. A child is born into a world that has changed faster than the parents can accept. While the heart of the parent beats in tradition, the spirit of the child breathes in modern air. The conflict is not about love; it is about fear. Fear of dishonor, fear of whispers, fear of being questioned.

And so, support is withheld not because it is absent, but because courage is. The tragedy is that everyone suffers. Parents feel crushed by imagined eyes, and children feel suffocated by unseen chains.

The Inherited Burden of Unlived Lives

In many families, especially across generations, mothers and grandmothers were never truly asked what *they* wanted from life. Their world was drawn by responsibility; not choice. They were taught to learn chores, marry at the "right" time, serve their in-laws, raise children, and finally, prepare for their old age surrounded by grandchildren.

In this long, rigid journey, they were never taught that life is meant to be lived, not merely endured. Their existence revolved around fulfilling expectations; not their own dreams. And when someone spends a lifetime ignoring their own self, they begin to search for that lost fulfillment in their children.

What they call "*sacrifice*" often carries the unspoken pain of unlived joy. So, without realizing it, they burden the next generation with the responsibility of making their story meaningful. The child becomes not just a person, but the vessel for the parent's unmet dreams.

But love cannot breathe when it is tangled with expectations. It can only thrive when both generations learn to set each other free.

The Unseen Ledger of Expectations

No one writes down its expectations in ink.
They live in the pauses after a child speaks, in the raised eyebrow when choices do not match the "normal," in the sighs of disappointment disguised as concern.
This is how an **unseen ledger** is born; where every dream, every step, every thought of the child is quietly measured against what should have been.

At first, this ledger is light. A good grade here, a polite smile there, a few adjustments to keep the elders happy. It feels harmless; even noble. But slowly, almost without warning, the weight grows. The child begins to walk carefully, not because the path is dangerous, but because every misstep leaves a mark in that invisible book.

"You have changed."
"This is not what we raised you to be."
"Think about us before yourself."

These are not cruel words. They are heavy ones. They carry the weight of generations who learned to survive by being accepted, not by being free. And in many homes, that survival instinct still speaks louder than love.

Some children learn to fold themselves into the narrow boxes of approval. Others resist, but the battle leaves them scarred. In either case, something precious is lost; the ability to breathe without asking permission.

The Inheritance of Guilt

One of the cruelest inheritances passed down through families is not wealth, not culture, but guilt.
Not the guilt of doing wrong; but the guilt of simply existing differently.

Parents often believe they are protecting their children. What they do not see is how protection, when rooted in fear, quietly becomes a cage. When a young mind is constantly told what will "make everyone proud," it stops asking what will make *itself* happy.
The child learns that peace is not a right but a reward; something granted only when they comply.

And so, begins the life of silent bargains:
"I will give up my dream if you are happy."
"I will silence my pain so you can smile at the relatives."
"I will live your version of me, even if I disappear inside."

Years later, that guilt does not fade. It matures. It settles into the bones, showing up in every hesitation, every unspoken word, every relationship where they feel they must *earn* love instead of simply *being worthy of it.*

When Love is Conditional

Love should be a shelter. But when soaked in expectations, it becomes a contract with invisible clauses. Support is offered, but only if you choose the "right" career, marry the "right" person, follow the "right" rules.

The tragedy is that both sides believe they are right.
The family says, "We love you and want the best for you."
The child whispers, "But the best for me isn't what you imagine."

This is the unbridgeable silence; where love speaks two different languages. One built on protection, the other on freedom. Both are valid, yet both collide.

And in the middle of this collision stands a soul; torn between being a dutiful child and a free human being. This is where depression often begins: not in rebellion, but in quiet suffocation.

When Love Becomes a Debt

In almost every culture, parents are seen as gods on earth. Their love is often called the only truly selfless one. And in many ways, it *is*; they give without pause, they protect, they sacrifice in ways words can't fully hold. But sometimes, love that begins as a gift quietly turns into a debt without anyone meaning it to.

Many children grow up hearing:

"We gave you everything."
"We sacrificed so much."
"We did not abandon you like others did."
"I bore the pain of bringing you into this world."

These words are rarely spoken to hurt. Often, they rise in moments of fear, frustration, or exhaustion. Yet for the child, they echo differently; not as love, but as a **reminder of a burden they never chose**.

A child never asked to be born; it was the parents' act of hope, faith, and love that brought them into this world. And if that act was a choice of love, then love should remain a gift; not a bargain.

When love turns into something that must be *repaid*, it loses the very purity it began with. The child, who once saw their parents as their safe haven, starts to feel like a debtor in their own home. Not because the parents are wrong; but because the language of love changed from *nurture* to *obligation*.

True selfless love, perhaps, lies not in reminding someone of what has been given... but in allowing them the freedom to live the life they were born for. In knowing that their joy, their freedom, their choices; do not erase the sacrifices, but **honor them**.

"Love is a seed, not a chain. When planted, it grows; when weighed down, it withers. True love does not keep score – it gives, and lets live."

The Turning Silence

At first, the child pleads; for understanding, for time, for trust.
Then comes the negotiation.

Then the guilt.
And finally, silence.

Silence does not mean acceptance. It means exhaustion. It means a heart that has spent too long trying to be heard in a house that listens only through the filter of expectation.

And in that silence, dreams begin to fade. Not with drama, but with quiet surrender.

This is the silent weight of expectations; not loud, not violent, but deeply binding. And this is why many people live lives that look perfect from the outside yet feel unbearable from within. Because love, when tied to conditions, can feel heavier than hate.

Story Time
Meera's Last Wish

The house was full of people, voices hushed, feet moving carefully. Children, grandchildren, even great-grandchildren had gathered around Meera's bed. At ninety, her frame was fragile, her breath uneven, her eyes distant. To them, she was slipping into memory; one more elder completing the circle of life.

But inside, her mind was not with them. It had traveled back seventy years, to a riverbank where the monsoon clouds had once poured their secrets over two trembling hearts.

"Arjun..." The name slipped past her lips, cracked and faint. Some of her children exchanged puzzled looks. They had never heard that name before.

The Forgotten Beginning

At nineteen, Meera had been like any other young girl of her time; dutiful, quiet, taught to keep her head bowed and her heart restrained. But there was one thing her family had not restrained: her walks to the library. And it was there that she first noticed Arjun.

He wasn't like the others. While the town's boys laughed loudly in tea stalls, Arjun sat at the corner table, scribbling furiously into notebooks. His clothes were simple, his pockets nearly empty, but his eyes; his eyes carried something Meera had never seen before: fire.

One afternoon, as she returned a book, a folded piece of paper slipped from its pages. A poem. Rough, uneven handwriting, but words that made her cheeks burn. *"The world tells me to bow, but my heart only knows how to rise. And in your silence, I hear the sound of freedom."*

She knew it was his. And from that day, their secret world began.

The Banyan Tree

By the river stood a banyan tree, its roots deep, its branches vast, shielding them from the world. That tree became their cathedral. Letters exchanged in trembling hands, stolen glances, whispered dreams.

One evening, as the rain soaked the earth, Arjun took her hand. His grip was firm, desperate. "Meera, run away with me. Tonight. We'll leave this town, live with little but live free. You'll write with me, travel with me... be mine without chains."

Her heart thundered. For a moment, she imagined it; the muddy road beneath her feet, his hand never letting go, the world fading behind them. But then came the sound of her father's voice in memory: *"A daughter's honor is not hers alone. She carries the weight of the family."*

Her lips trembled. "Arjun... I can't."

Something in his eyes shattered. He released her hand. The rain fell harder, blurring his figure as he walked away. She never saw him again.

A Life Fulfilled, A Soul Empty

Meera's marriage was arranged swiftly. Her husband was kind, stable, respected. He gave her a house, security, children. Festivals filled the home with laughter, neighbors praised her for her grace, relatives envied her fate.

On the surface, her life was whole. But at night, when everyone slept, she would sit by the window, staring at the stars, and wonder if Arjun was out there somewhere; writing, living, remembering.

Years turned into decades. She never spoke his name, never breathed his memory aloud. But inside, the silence grew like a shadow that never left her side.

Her husband passed, her children grew, grandchildren came. She smiled in photographs, blessed birthdays, whispered prayers. But sometimes, when a sudden breeze rattled the window, she felt nineteen again, standing beneath the banyan tree, watching the rain take away the only part of her that had ever been truly hers.

The Last Wish

Now, as her family gathered in her final hours, she was no longer in her home; she was back at the riverbank, soaked in rain, heart pounding. Her lips parted. "Arjun..."

Her children leaned closer, confused. "Who is Arjun?" one of them whispered.

Her voice was faint, but clear enough to silence the room. "If you love... don't wait. Don't surrender to fear, or to names, or to society. I let go once... and I died that day. My body only followed much later."

Tears rolled down her sunken cheeks. Her eyes closed, a soft smile lingering as if she could finally see the boy with ink-stained fingers again.

Her family wept around her, believing they had lost her. But the truth was, they had never fully known her. The woman they mourned had lived among them, but the girl who loved by the banyan tree had been buried long ago, beneath the heavy soil of expectation.

"To breathe is not always to live. To obey is not always to belong. And the deepest tragedies are not in what we lose, but in what we never dared to keep."

Reflection

There are lives that look complete from the outside, yet within them lie silent graves of unspoken dreams. For some it is a love never lived, for others a passion never pursued, a voice never heard, a journey never taken. Expectations often bury these desires so gently that even we forget where they once lived inside us; until regret digs them out in our quietest hours. The true sorrow is not in failing, but in never having tried, in never allowing the soul to stretch its own wings. And when the final curtain falls, the heaviest silence is not death itself, but the haunting echo of the life we could have lived.

"The world may forgive rebellion, but it never returns lost time. And the heaviest coffin is not made of wood, but of unfulfilled dreams carried to the grave."

Chapter 3
The Vicious Circle Within

How self-doubt grows into a chain reaction; overthinking, guilt, self-blame. The karmic bondage of thoughts that trap us in a cycle of fear.

The Unheard Conversations

"I could see my mind turning over the same questions, the same doubts, until I forgot what freedom felt like."

– 34-year-old entrepreneur

"Every time I tried to trust my own choice, I felt invisible hands pulling me back into fear, guilt, and second-guessing."

– late 20s, creative professional

"It's like a shadow I cannot shake; every thought, every feeling, bouncing back, trapping me in myself."

– 40-year-old, corporate manager

"My mind became a maze,
Every turn leading back to the start.
Questions became knives,
Each cutting deeper than the last.
I was judge and prisoner,
Guard and captive.
And the more I struggled,
The tighter the chains became."

The Circle No One Sees

The deepest struggles of life often go unseen, because they unfold not in the outside world, but within the labyrinth of the mind. There are no witnesses, no applause for resilience, no sympathy for invisible battles. And yet, the wounds of thought often cut deeper than the sharpest sword.

This circle begins innocently enough; with a doubt. A misstep. A rejection. Someone's harsh word. A failed attempt. The mind seizes it, and instead of letting it pass like a cloud, it roots it firmly in memory. From that seed grows a question: "*What if I am not enough?*"

The question circles back on itself. "*If I failed once, maybe I will fail again. If they disapproved once, maybe I am unworthy always.*" Every doubt feeds the next. The mind becomes its own courtroom: it raises accusations, produces evidence, passes judgment, and then chains itself in the very prison it has built.

And thus begins the vicious circle: overthinking, guilt, self-blame, fear. The wheel keeps spinning, faster with every turn.

The Karmic bondage of Thought

Ancient wisdom often spoke of karma not just as actions, but as the subtle impressions left upon the soul. Thoughts, too, are a kind of karma. Each thought is a seed, and like seeds, they multiply.

Think of it this way: a single fear is like a drop of ink in clear water. Alone, it may seem small. But the more you stir it, the more it spreads, until the entire vessel is tinted. Fear breeds hesitation. Hesitation leads to inaction. Inaction breeds regret. Regret strengthens fear.

Thus, the bondage of thought is not imaginary; it is karmic in the truest sense. It ties the present to the past and stretches into the future, binding us with invisible ropes. Every choice not made, every silence kept, every step delayed; all become links in a chain forged by our own mind.

What is most painful is not the weight of one thought, but the way one thought breeds another, until the soul is caught in a web of its own weaving.

Understanding Anekantvad: The Blindness of Absolutes

Why does this circle feel so unbreakable? Because we often mistake one angle of reality for the whole truth.

Jain philosophy speaks of *Anekantvad*; the doctrine of pluralism. It tells us that nothing is absolute, that reality has countless sides. A mountain may appear still and lifeless from afar, yet teem with rivers, trees, and wild animals when seen up close. A diamond looks dull from one side, dazzling from another.

So too with life. What appears as failure from one angle may be preparation from another. What seems rejection in one moment may be redirection in another. A wound can feel like destruction, but in another light, it becomes the very space where growth can begin.

But in the grip of self-doubt, we forget this. We cling to one perspective; the harshest one; and declare it the whole truth. "*I failed, therefore I am a failure.*" "*They rejected me, therefore I am unworthy.*"

This is the blindness of absolutes: the refusal to see that truth is never one-faced. Life is not a straight line of right or wrong; it is a mosaic of perspectives, all of which hold a piece of the real.

Anekantvad is not just philosophy; it is medicine for the vicious circle. It reminds us that no thought, no judgment, no fear is the *entire* truth. The circle tightens only when we deny other possibilities. The moment we admit that reality has more than one face, the chain begins to loosen.

Escaping the loop of self doubt

If you have ever lain awake at night, you know the spiral:

- One thought enters.
- It splits into two questions.
- The questions multiply into what-ifs.
- The what-ifs summon fear.
- Fear summons guilt.
- Guilt whispers: "*You are not enough.*"

And the spiral deepens.

This cycle feels karmic because it feeds itself. You wake up tired from the weight of thoughts. You avoid decisions, fearing mistakes. The avoidance becomes a mistake itself, leading to more guilt, more thoughts. And soon, the mind becomes both stage and audience of its own endless drama.

What we rarely notice is that overthinking does not seek truth; it seeks certainty. But life, by its nature, is uncertain. No amount of spinning thoughts will solve it. Certainty is not found by thinking more, but by learning to live with multiple truths, multiple angles; the very essence of *Anekantvad.*

To break this cycle, one does not need grand answers. One needs perspective. A single shift can weaken the chain.

When guilt whispers, "*You failed,*" remind yourself: failure is one view, growth is another.
When fear insists, "*You will fall again,*" respond: perhaps, but even falling is learning.
When regret says, "*It's too late,*" ask: too late for what? Too late in one path may be the beginning of another.

The mind's prison feeds on singularity; on insisting there is only one meaning to every event. But when we learn to see life through many windows, the prison doors begin to open.

"A single truth can bind you, but many truths can set you free. To see life from only one angle is to live in chains; to embrace its many faces is to remember that freedom was always within."

Chapter 4
The Faces of Depression

Depression as lived reality: frustration, anger, seeking validation, and losing confidence when choices are constantly invalidated.

The Unheard Conversations

"People tell me to smile, but no one sees the ache beneath the teeth, the heaviness behind the eyes."

– 36-year-old, married

"I learned that depression isn't absence of happiness; it's living a life everyone thinks is fine while your soul is quietly breaking."

– late 20s, young mother

"Even in a crowd, I felt invisible. Even when loved, I felt unheard. It is the emptiness that terrifies."

– 32-year-old, creative professional

"Depression wore many masks;
A smile at dinner,
A tear on the pillow,
An emptiness between crowds.
I lived in rehearsed laughter,
But my soul spoke in silence.
No one saw the storm,
For I carried it inside."

Depression is not the absence of life, but the drowning of it; a soul screaming beneath the noise of the world, unheard, unseen, yet unbearably alive in pain.

The Silent Visitor

Depression does not arrive with noise; it tiptoes in softly, almost politely, until you realize it has unpacked its bags inside you. At first, it is barely noticed; a little tiredness, a passing sadness, a hesitation in joy. But slowly, it grows roots. It begins to color the mornings, hollow the evenings, and turn the nights into endless watches of thought.

The tragedy of depression is not only in its weight but in its invisibility. The world sees your face, but not your storm. It hears your words, but not your silence. You laugh on cue, respond when spoken to, move through your duties; but inside, something collapses each day.

And because the collapse is hidden, no one rushes to help. People explain their struggles, their needs, their stories. But who listens long enough to notice that your own soul is breaking?

Frustration: The First Flame

Frustration is often the first mask of depression. It begins with small irritations; *Why can't things be different? Why can't I be understood? Why is my effort invisible?*
At first, it is directed outward: at family, at society, at circumstances. But soon, it turns inward.

Maybe I am the problem. Maybe I am not enough. Maybe my voice has no weight.

This frustration simmers like fire without release. It makes small tasks heavy, small delays unbearable.
A forgotten message, a neglected word, a passing judgment; all burn like salt in wounds already open.

Often, in this stage, the sufferer says things like;

"You don't understand me."
"I'm tired of explaining myself."
"Nothing ever feels right anymore."

But these statements, instead of being heard as pain, are taken as disrespect, moodiness, or ingratitude. The listener defends, argues, corrects; unaware that the person before them is fighting tears, not trying to win a debate.

The world sees only irritation. Inside, it is despair trying to find a voice.
And each time that voice is silenced or dismissed, the flame grows hotter; until frustration becomes the first quiet fire of hopelessness.

Anger: The Loud Silence

When frustration finds no ear, it mutates into anger.
But not always the shouting, breaking, storming kind.
Often, it is the quiet anger; the tightened chest, the restless pacing, the silent screams behind closed doors.

Anger in depression is misunderstood. People see only rebellion; they miss the ache beneath.

It is not hatred, but helplessness in disguise.
It is the sound of a soul banging on the walls of its own cage, whispering, "*Please listen before I stop speaking at all.*"

A sufferer might say;

"Just leave me alone for a while."
"You'll never understand what I'm going through."
"I don't care anymore."

But what they really mean is;

"I want peace, but I don't know how to find it."
"I wish someone could sit beside me without fixing me."
"I am not angry at you; I'm angry that I don't know how to live anymore."

Yet their tone sounds distant, sharp, unpredictable. Loved ones react with confusion or hurt; they walk away, defend themselves, or label it as "attitude."
And in that moment, a gulf widens.
The anger grows louder inside but quieter outside, turning into exhaustion.
Burn others, and relationships suffer; burn self, and the soul begins to crumble.

Anger, when unheard, becomes the silence before collapse.

The Hunger for Validation

Perhaps one of the cruelest faces of depression is the desperate search for validation.
When your choices are constantly questioned, your

emotions minimized, your worth measured by obedience; the soul begins to starve.

Every action becomes a silent question:
"Am I enough? Do you see me? Do I matter?"

The sufferer may say;

"I don't think I'm doing anything right."
"Do you even care if I'm here?"
"I just wanted you to be proud of me."

But instead of being met with empathy, these words often trigger arguments:

"Why are you so negative?"
"You always make it about yourself."
"We've done everything for you; what more do you want?"

Each response, though perhaps well-meant, pushes the person deeper into shame.
They stop asking questions. They stop explaining. They simply start withdrawing.

Validation becomes addictive. One kind word from someone can lift their spirit like oxygen to fire; but the relief is fleeting. The emptiness returns, demanding more. They begin to live through borrowed mirrors, seeing themselves only through others' eyes. But every mirror they borrow is cracked; reflecting fragments, never the whole.

And one day, they stop looking altogether.

When frustration, anger, and the hunger for validation coexist, the person lives in emotional turbulence;

oscillating between wanting to be seen and wanting to disappear. They crave understanding but fear judgment. They long for connection but no longer trust it.
And the tragedy is; while everyone sees their behavior, no one sees their pain.

The Shattering of Confidence

Confidence does not vanish all at once. It cracks slowly, like glass under pressure. At first, it is subtle; an ignored opinion here, a corrected choice there, a small shame planted in fertile soil. Over time, these tiny fractures deepen. One day you find yourself hesitating over even the simplest decisions: *What if I am wrong again? What if I hurt someone? What if I disappoint?* The questions repeat like a mantra, until the doubt feels louder than your own voice.

The child who once played freely becomes the adult who second-guesses every step. The laughter that once erupted naturally becomes rehearsed, carefully timed to match the room. The curiosity that once led you to climb trees or speak without fear now waits for permission. This is not merely a loss of joy; it is a loss of self. Confidence is not just a skill; it is the very belief that you deserve to exist in your own shape. When it breaks, life becomes a series of calculations. Every choice feels like a cliff, every word like a risk.

And this loss is more than sadness; it is paralysis. The person knows they are alive but feels unable to live, as though life has become a performance, they no longer auditioned for but must continue. They are not only afraid of failing others; they are afraid of failing themselves, of confirming the quiet suspicion that they have already failed.

The Emptiness Between Crowds

People often mistake depression for loneliness, but loneliness is simple; it's the absence of people. Depression is crueler; it is the absence of connection *within* presence. You could be at a wedding, surrounded by laughter and music, yet feel as though you're sealed behind glass. You can hug someone and feel nothing. You can talk for hours and feel unheard. The echo inside grows louder than the voices outside.

It is the ache of being unseen, even when looked at. The pain of being unheard, even when spoken to. The haunting thought that you could disappear, and the world would continue unchanged. This isn't drama; it's an internal reality. It feels as if you're drifting further from shore, waving as loudly as you can, and nobody sees you slipping under.

And this emptiness has weight. It presses on the chest, fogs the mind, drains the spirit. It's not a sharp pain; it's a dull, constant ache that makes even breathing feel heavy. It whispers: "*You do not belong. You do not matter. You are invisible.*" And after hearing that whisper for too long, part of you starts to believe it.

Sometimes, in a crowd, you smile. Not because you're happy, but because it hides the hollowness. Sometimes, you become the most cheerful person in the room, because it distracts from your own void. But when the crowd disperses and silence returns, the emptiness floods back like water through a broken dam.

The Spiral of the Worst

Unchecked, depression deepens into something darker. It no longer feels like sadness; sadness at least has tears, an outlet, a kind of warmth. This is numbness. A grey fog where nothing tastes, nothing moves, nothing matters. It is a hunger that refuses food, a thirst that cannot be quenched, an exhaustion that no sleep cures.

At its worst, depression feeds thoughts of escape. Not always out of hatred for life, but out of weariness with the weight of living. It's not rebellion; it's resignation. The idea of ending it feels less like a violent act and more like putting down a heavy bag after carrying it for too long. People on the outside mistake this for weakness. But in truth, it is not weakness; it is the slow depletion of strength, drained by a battle no one else could see.

This is the darkest mask of depression: the silence before surrender. It is not always dramatic; sometimes it's a quiet giving up, a slow dimming of presence. And because it's quiet, it is often missed; until it's too late. Lives are lost here, not because they lacked courage, but because their courage was stretched beyond human measure.

The Unseen Storm

Depression is not one face but many. Frustration. Anger. Hunger. Emptiness. Silence. Each mask hides the same wound: the longing to be seen, to be heard, to be allowed to exist without judgment.

It is not weakness, nor selfishness, nor drama. It is the human soul collapsing under invisible weights. And like any storm, it does not pass by command. It needs shelter, patience, and most of all, recognition.

For the cruelest thing depression does is convince the sufferer that they are alone, when in truth, countless others carry the same hidden storm.

"Depression is not the end of life; it is the cry of life itself, begging to be lived differently. To heal it is not to silence the storm, but to remember that storms pass, and skies; no matter how dark; were always meant to clear."

Story Time
The Weight of Being Loved

The city was still half-asleep when Aanya unlocked her apartment door.
It was 7:15 a.m.; she had been up all night finalizing a report.
The coffee on her desk had turned cold, untouched like most things in her life lately.

Her phone vibrated.
Maa: "Good morning, beta. Your cousin got promoted! So proud of him. He's buying a car now. When will you think of settling?"

Aanya smiled faintly, though her throat ached.
She had received her own promotion last month; no celebration, no call of pride, just silence.
When she mentioned it once, her mother had said, "*Of course, you did well. You always do. We raised you right.*"

The credit was never hers. The fault always was.

Where Pride Lived Louder Than Peace

Aanya's parents were not cruel; they were ordinary.
Ordinary enough to care more about *what people said* than *what their daughter felt.*

Her father used to call her every evening when she first moved to the city for work. He would talk about his day,

his friends, his health; small things that made her feel anchored.
But slowly, the calls stopped.

When she called instead, he'd sigh.

"You always call at the wrong time, Aanya. You know your mother's blood pressure rises after talking about your career stress. Why don't you find something stable? Get married and relax. Life isn't about running all the time."

And just like that, guilt replaced connection.
Even her voice became heavy; afraid to cause discomfort, even to her own parents.

They loved her; but only when her success looked respectable and her struggles stayed hidden.

The Moon Forgot Her Light

Rohan entered her life like a calm after storm.
He was attentive, passionate, protective; everything she thought she needed.
He loved her deeply, and she loved him for it.

But love, when misunderstood, can become a leash disguised as safety.

At first, he admired her ambition.
Later, he resented it.

"You're too busy for me these days. Earlier, you used to text all the time. Now I have to fight for your attention."

She tried explaining, "*It's just a phase, Rohan. Things will settle soon. I just need some time.*"

"You have changed, Aanya. You are colder now. Is this really what you want? A career that makes you forget to feel?"

His words always came wrapped in concern, but they carried accusation underneath.

He would fight, threaten to leave, and when she broke down crying, he would hold her again, whispering,

"I cannot live without you. Just do not push me away again."

It was love, yes; but love that demanded she stay small, manageable, and pliant.

She was not loved for who she was; but for how she could make others feel secure.

The Gradual Unraveling

Aanya tried harder. For everyone.
She laughed louder at family gatherings, smiled brighter on video calls, pretended enthusiasm at work.

Her mother would say,

"You should see how your cousin's wife balances everything. You should learn, Aanya."

Her boss would say,

"You're too emotional. You need to toughen up if you want to lead."

Rohan would say,

"I just miss the old you. The soft one."

And every time, she'd apologize; for changing, for trying, for simply existing differently.

The Breaking Point

One evening, Rohan came over after a fight the night before. She was sitting on the floor with her laptop, half-done report on the screen, tears staining the keyboard.

He walked in quietly.

"You've been crying again, haven't you?"

She wiped her face quickly.

"It's nothing. I am just tired."

"You always say that, Aanya. 'I'm tired.' When will this end?"

She wanted to say, *when someone finally stops asking me to be someone else.*
But she could not.

Instead, she whispered,

"Please, just be patient with me. Once this project ends, once my family settles down, once I......."

"Once, once, once!" he interrupted. "Everything with you is a waiting game. What about now? Don't I deserve happiness too?"

Her silence was her answer.

He sighed, rubbed his forehead, and muttered,

"You know I love you, right? But I can't keep doing this if you keep shutting me out."

And as he left, she realized: *everyone loves the version of you that doesn't inconvenience them.*

The Quiet Collapse

Weeks passed. Her health worsened. She forgot meals, lost sleep, lived in a fog.
Even music; once her solace; began to sound hollow.

Her mother called again.

"Your father's not keeping well. You should visit. And please, dress nicely this time. The neighbors talk, you know."

Her father, in the background:

"Tell her to book a morning train. It's safer for girls."

Aanya nodded silently, tears in her eyes. They were worried; but never about her. Only about *how she looked, what people said, how it reflected on them.*

That night, she opened her journal.
The last entry she'd written months ago read:
"I want to make them proud."

She turned to a blank page and began to write again.

"I wish pride and love weren't always measured by obedience.

I wish care didn't come with comparison.
I wish I didn't have to prove I'm worth loving."

The words trembled. So did her hands.

The Final Silence

The next morning, her mother kept calling; no answer.
Her boss texted; "Are you joining the meeting?"
Rohan messaged; "I'm sorry for last night. Let's fix this, please."

No replies.

When the door was finally opened by her neighbor that evening, the flat was still; eerily peaceful.
The coffee cup half-finished, laptop open on a draft email that read:
"I tried to make everyone happy, but I forgot what my own happiness felt like."

The Aftermath

Her family cried for days. Her mother fainted repeatedly, whispering,

"We just wanted what was best for her."

Rohan sat alone in the hospital corridor, his hands trembling, whispering,

"I should've been patient. I should've stayed."

The boss sent flowers. The company released a short condolence email; "A *valuable employee, gone too soon."*

But none of them truly understood that Aanya didn't die because she was unloved.
She died because her love was conditional; everywhere she turned.

Aanya's story isn't one of villains or victims.
Everyone in her life loved her; but for *their own comfort, validation, image, or control.*
No one loved her freely, for who she truly was beneath her fatigue, beneath her fear, beneath her quiet rebellion to stay gentle in a world that rewarded hardness.

She didn't want to die.
She just wanted, for once, to stop explaining why she was worth being loved without earning it.

"Sometimes, love doesn't kill; it suffocates.
Not by hatred, but by hands that hold too tightly.
And when you finally let go, the world calls it tragedy.
But maybe... it was just the first breath of freedom."

The Man Who Spoke to Walls

Arun was forty-seven when silence began to take root inside him.

It did not happen overnight. It began the way dust gathers; quietly, invisibly, until one day you realize everything is covered in it.

For most of his life, Arun had been the kind of man others relied on. The dependable son who carried his family through his father's long illness, the employee who never said no, the friend who remembered birthdays even when his own went unnoticed. His life was a sequence of responsibilities, neatly arranged like files on his office desk.

But somewhere in those years of doing what was right, he forgot what felt true. He had dreams once; small, harmless dreams. He wanted to paint, to travel alone, to write letters that did not begin with "as per our last discussion." But life taught him that duty came first, that desires were luxuries meant for younger, freer souls.

Then his mother passed away, and with her, the last person who ever asked, "How are you, really?"

After the funeral, everyone moved on with the efficiency of the living. But something inside Arun did not follow. He continued to work, to laugh when required, but his voice began to lose color, like photographs fading under sunlight.

At first, he thought it was tiredness.

Then he stopped answering calls. Then, gradually, even the calls stopped coming. The silence felt both cruel and comforting; like being forgotten and finally understood at once.

He did not hate people. He simply no longer knew what to say. Words, once his currency, now felt expensive. Every conversation required energy he did not possess. He spent evenings staring at the ceiling fan, watching it spins endlessly; the same circle, the same noise. His mind was like that fan: moving constantly but going nowhere.

He used to call it thinking time.

But weeks passed, and he realized he had not thought anything new in months. Just repeated the same silent sentences:

You should be stronger.

You have no reason to be sad.

Others have it worse.

Depression had not come crashing down; it had settled over him, like dusk.

One evening, his daughter, Mira, came home early from college. She found him standing in the balcony, speaking softly to the wall. His tone was calm, almost conversational, as if explaining something. She froze, unsure whether to interrupt. Finally, she asked, "*Papa... who are you talking to?*"

Arun looked up, startled, and then smiled faintly. "*The wall listens*," he said. "It does not advise. It does not judge. It just stays."

He was not wrong.

The following weeks blurred together. His family tried everything; temples, doctors, cheerful dinners, motivational talks from well-meaning friends. But nothing touched the core of it. What no one saw was that Arun did not want to die; he just wanted the noise to stop. The noise of expectation, the noise of self-reproach, the noise of being endlessly needed but never known.

One morning, Mira left a small sticky note on the wall. It said simply:

"I'm here. You can talk to me too."

When Arun saw it, he did not cry. He just sat down quietly, staring at those words as if they were sunlight in a room long locked. It was such a small thing; a scrap of paper; but something inside him shifted.

The wall was no longer just a wall. It was a bridge.

That evening, he began to write. Not long letters or confessions; just a few words every night. Fragments. Memories. Regrets. Slowly, the words formed sentences, and the sentences began to carry his pain away from the walls and back into the world.

Healing did not arrive like dawn; it arrived like dusk; slowly, tenderly, teaching him that even darkness can hold a kind of peace.

Part II

The Unfolding Within

Chapter- 5

The Turning Point – No One Can Save You but You

The world may hold your hands, but it cannot walk your path. Healing begins when you stop waiting to be rescued, and start learning to return home; to yourself.

The Unheard Conversations

"I realized that no amount of advice, pills, or encouragement could fill the hollow space inside; only I could."

– *mid-30s, former burnout survivor*

"It was terrifying to accept that I was my own anchor; and yet, it was the first time I felt the stirrings of freedom."

– *29-year-old, struggling with anxiety*

"The world will not pause; the people will not change. But for the first time, I could decide who I am."

– *31-year-old professional*

There came a moment when the mirror no longer frightened me,
when I stopped asking, "Who will fix me?"
and whispered instead, "What if I can?"
The same eyes that once searched for help
now learned to hold their own reflection with kindness.
And in that gaze, I met the only savior I ever needed; me.

The Myth of Rescue

From childhood, we are taught that help always comes from outside; a parent, a teacher, a friend, a god. Someone will guide, fix, heal, or at least listen. And for a time, it works. The world feels safer when we believe someone is watching over us.

But as life deepens, we begin to see the truth that no one tells us early enough: no one can live your pain for you. People can stand at the edge of your storm, but they cannot step inside it. Their umbrellas may keep them dry, but the rain that soaks you is yours alone.

When we fall apart, our first instinct is to look outward; to doctors, to therapy, to loved ones. And yes, each has its place. A kind listener can open a window in your darkness. Medication can soften the edge of unbearable nights. Yet, if the heart remains unhealed, if the root remains untouched, the same pain returns; quieter, deeper, more entangled.

The truth is simple but difficult to accept:
No one can pull you out until you stop waiting to be saved. Healing is not an act of rescue; it is an act of reclamation; reclaiming the lost relationship between *you and yourself.*

In Jain philosophy, the soul; the *jiva*; carries its own energy, its own karmic imprints. It is both the bearer and the liberator of its burdens. No external savior can erase those bonds; only awareness can. This isn't punishment; it is empowerment. Because if your pain is your own, your freedom is too.

The Lost Relationship; You and Yourself

There comes a time when we realize that we have become strangers to our own hearts. We know what others like about us, what they expect from us, but not who we truly are.
We speak, but not from ourselves.
We act, but mostly to fit the image of what is "right."
We survive, but forget how to live.

You ask yourself quietly, "*When was the last time I truly heard my own voice?*"
And the silence that follows feels heavier than any noise.

This loss of connection does not happen suddenly; it dissolves slowly, like color fading from an old photograph. Every time we choose to please others over our peace, every time we silence our truth to maintain harmony, a part of us disappears.
Until one day, you wake up and realize; you have built a life where your presence is optional.

Rebuilding that relationship is the essence of healing. You must learn to sit with yourself; to listen, not to judge. To forgive, not to escape. To look within and say, "*I see you. I know it hurts. But I'm here now.*"

Jainism calls this awareness *Anekantavāda*; the principle that truth is many-sided. Nothing in this world has only one interpretation, one reality, or one cause. Similarly, you are not defined by a single mistake, a single failure, or a single perception of others.
To embrace Anekantavāda in your healing means to accept

that your pain, your choices, your regrets; all are fragments of a bigger, evolving truth. None define your entirety.

When you stop seeing yourself through one rigid lens; "I am broken," "I am unworthy," "I failed"; you allow space for other truths to breathe: *"I am learning." "I am trying." "I am still alive."*

Acceptance: The Door to Liberation

Acceptance is not surrender. It is seeing things as they are, not as we wish them to be. It is stepping out of the argument with life.

We often waste years fighting what has already happened; replaying conversations, rewriting endings, blaming fate, or waiting for closure. But nothing changes until we stop resisting. Pain, like a guest, stays longer when we keep denying its presence.

When you finally say, "Yes, it hurt. It still does. But I accept it," something miraculous happens. The energy you once used to resist begins to heal you instead.

In Jain practice, there is *Samayik*; a state of equanimity, where you pause the motion of judgment and see life from a still point. For even ten minutes, you detach from the roles, the noise, the reactions. You simply *observe*.
This observation itself starts loosening the karmic knots; the mental habits that keep you chained to pain.

Try this: when you feel the storm within, sit quietly.
Do not say, "I am sad." Instead, say, "There is sadness."

Do not say, "I am angry." Instead, say, "There is anger." You are not the emotion; you are the one witnessing it.

This shift; from being to observing; is the first doorway to liberation.

Building Your Own World

Once you begin to see clearly, the next step is reconstruction; not of your house, your job, or your relationships, but of your inner world.

We often think healing means changing everything around us. But transformation begins quietly; in the smallest decisions made in honesty.

Wake up and make your bed; not for productivity, but for peace.
Write something that feels true; not perfect, just honest.
Step outside, even if for a few breaths of sunlight.
Eat food because your body deserves care, not punishment.

These small acts whisper to your subconscious: *I am choosing myself again.*

Building your world does not mean rebellion. It means choosing alignment. You can stay within the same circumstances, yet live differently. Because the shift is not in the scenery; it's in sight.

As Jain karma theory teaches, energy follows awareness. Each thought, word, and action carries vibration; subtle, invisible threads that weave our reality. When you choose peace in small moments, you untie threads of past pain. You change the texture of your inner karma.

The Strength to Begin Again

There will be days when strength feels impossible. When it feels easier to stay broken than to try. On those days, remember: progress is not a straight road; it's a spiral. You may visit the same pain again, but each time, you see it from a higher point.

Discipline becomes devotion when done with compassion. Getting up is victory. Trying again is prayer.

When Jainism speaks of purification, it is not about rituals; it's about awareness. Every conscious act; forgiveness, patience, silence; scrubs a layer of karmic dust. The more you act with awareness, the lighter your soul becomes.

You begin to feel energy where exhaustion once lived.
You begin to notice calm where chaos used to reign.
This is not magic; it is the science of self-realization.

Love as Self-Liberation

You may have spent years searching for love; in approval, in people, in places. But true love begins when you stop demanding it from others and begin offering it to yourself.

To love yourself is to forgive the versions of you that did not know better; the one who begged to be heard, who stayed when it hurt, who trusted too easily, who gave without balance. Each was doing their best with what they knew then.

Ahimsa, the Jain principle of non-violence, starts here; with your own thoughts. Every time you tell yourself, "I am not enough," you harm your own spirit. Every time you say, "I forgive you," you heal it.

Love yourself as you would tend to a sacred flame; gently, patiently, knowing it may flicker but will never truly die.

The Rebirth of Inner Will

The moment you stop seeking motivation and start creating it, you are reborn. Healing does not mean you will never break again; it means you now know how to rebuild.

When silence becomes peace instead of punishment, you have evolved.
When solitude becomes strength instead of loneliness, you have awakened.
When pain becomes teacher instead of enemy, you have transcended.

This is where the cycle of karma begins to dissolve. Awareness replaces reaction. Compassion replaces control. And you finally realize; you were never meant to be saved. You were meant to awaken.

There is a day that comes quietly, without thunder or revelation.
You wake up, and something inside feels lighter.
The memories still exist, the world is still imperfect; but your heart no longer trembles.
You look at your reflection and see not a survivor, but a being becoming whole.

The world has not changed.
But you have.
And that is enough.

"No one can walk your path,
but once you start walking,
the universe begins to clear the stones from your way."

Bridging the Reflection and the Release

Understanding this truth changes the rhythm of our suffering.

We stop asking "*Why don't they understand me?*" and begin whispering "*Maybe they, too, are trying to be understood.*"

This subtle shift does not erase the pain, but it lightens its hold; for empathy, even towards those who hurt us, becomes a quiet liberation.

The moment we stop waiting for mirrors, we start meeting our true self. And that is where healing begins; not in someone's apology, not in their approval, but in the silence where we finally see our own worth without needing validation.

It is the moment the prisoner realizes that the key was always inside the cage.

Because no one can truly save us but ourselves;

not because others do not care,

but because the door of healing only opens from the inside.

The Mirror of Understanding: The World May Not Change but You Still Can

When we are in pain, all we truly want is to be understood. Not advised, not corrected; just understood.

But in that silent longing hides a truth we often overlook: the same way we ache for someone to see our pain, others too are waiting to be seen through their own chaos.

We keep expecting mirrors in human form; someone who will reflect our thoughts, our values, our intensity.

Yet no two souls share the same reflection; our lives are shaped by different storms, different skies, different fears. And when our reflection fails to appear, we call it *loneliness.*

But perhaps it's not loneliness at all; perhaps it is life reminding us that we were never meant to find our entire reflection in another.
We were meant to find *pieces* of ourselves in others, and the rest, in silence; in our own heart.

This is not to say that those who feel misunderstood are wrong, but to recognize that *understanding itself* is a two-way light.

When we seek to be seen, we must also dare to see.

When we crave empathy, we must remember that even those who hurt us are carrying invisible wars.

And sometimes, the peace we want from others is only possible when we stop demanding a mirror, and start being one.

"The Mirror That Never Lied"

I searched for myself in every face,
Every smile that promised grace.
But mirrors don't breathe, and hearts don't clone,
Each reflection was their own.

They too, perhaps, looked back at me,
Hoping my eyes would help them see.
Two souls calling through the haze;
Both lost in their different maze.

Now I stand still, without demand,
Understanding; like water, slips through the hand.
No one was meant to mirror me true,
For I was the mirror I always knew.

Chapter 6
Breaking the Cage

Freedom is not escape. It is understanding. The cage was never only iron; it was habits, fear, duty, and the small kindnesses that asked for price. To break it is not to punish those who built it, but to remember that every soul is born to learn its own lesson; and to choose, at last, to live by that lesson.

The Unheard Conversations

"When I finally named the cage, I could see it was built with love as much as expectation; and that understanding didn't lessen its weight, but it gave me courage."

– *35-year-old*

"I forgave not to let them off, but to release myself from the silent burden of carrying their fears and my guilt."

– *early 30s, working woman*

"Freedom was not a shout or a rebellion; it was a quiet decision, made day by day, to honor my own heart."

– *late 20s, young professional*

One morning, the river did not rush as it always had.
The same stones waited, patient and unmoved.
The walls still whispered their old names,
The sky still wore yesterday's shade of grey.

Yet something within me had softened.
The storm had not vanished; it had simply grown tired.
The voices still spoke, but gentler now,
As if they too had been waiting to be understood.

I realized the world had not changed;
It was I who had stopped running.
I looked at my own reflection,
And for the first time, did not turn away.

The key in my palm no longer felt like a burden,
But a quiet invitation;
To open the door,
And finally, step into myself.

The Realization of the Cage

The cage is seldom loud. It does not announce itself with drama or chains. It grows quietly, almost imperceptibly, from small things; a comment spoken as advice, a compliment that asks for repetition, a well-meaning suggestion that masks expectation. It is built by hands that love you, by voices that want to guide you, and by hearts that fear the unknown.

A woman looks out of a window one morning and notices that she has never chosen the colors of her days; the route she walks, the meals she eats, even the clothes she wears. A man in an office laughs at a joke that leaves no warmth in his chest, because the discomfort of silence feels heavier than the lie. A child learns quickly: smiles and affection are earned, not freely given, and love seems to arrive most easily when performance meets expectation.

And then; one quiet morning; the cage becomes visible. Seeing it does not break it instantly. The walls, the bars, the weight; they are still there. But now they can be named. And in naming them, there is a first taste of freedom.

Recognition is not blame. One can acknowledge the forces that shaped a life; fear, duty, scarcity, love constrained by its own limits; and still bow to the humanity of those who shaped them. Parents who insist on security are not cruel; they are frightened of the world and trying to protect. A partner who demands compliance is guarding against hurt, against being left. Society that praises conformity is trying to preserve order in a world it fears will spiral.

The cage exists alongside care. Understanding this softens the edges. Anger recedes, not entirely, but enough for a quieter courage to enter. For the first time, you realize that the prison was never built from malice. It was built from love, from fear, from human imperfection. And if it was built from these, perhaps it can be unraveled the same way; patiently, deliberately, with understanding and self-compassion.

The Quiet Revolution Within

True revolution is often silent. It begins with an inner question: *What if I allowed myself one honest choice today?* It does not demand a scream or a dramatic walkout. It asks for small rebellions: a single "no," a day of choosing what feels true, a refusal to edit the self for comfort.

In the quiet, two things happen. First, one learns to recognize the pattern of reaction: the learned reflex to apologize, to downplay, to make oneself smaller. Second, one practices a new reflex: to pause, to breathe, to check whether the response is coming from habit or heart.

This is not easy. The revolution asks you to risk a loved one's displeasure for the sake of your own voice. It asks that you tolerate the discomfort of being imperfect in others' eyes. There will be loss. There will be misunderstandings. But there will also be clarity.

A small scene will help: a daughter returns late from work; her mother's face tightens. Once, the daughter would say, "Sorry, Ma. Traffic." Now she pauses and says, "I stayed to finish the piece I was proud of." The words hang between them. The mother's disappointment and the daughter's truth both exist. The conversation may end in argument; it may end in silence. But the daughter's inner life begins to belong to her again.

The quiet revolution is humble. It invites practice: one minute of stillness in the morning, a single sentence of truth at dinner, a refusal to bend when tired. Over months, the small acts stitch a new identity. The self becomes accustomed to being consulted.

The Power of Detachment (*Aparigraha*)

Detachment is often misunderstood. It is not coldness or withdrawal. It is the art of holding lightly. In practice, it means loving without clinging, giving without demanding, and doing one's duty without making one's worth depend on the outcome.

The Jain teaching of *Aparigraha*; non-possessiveness; is a practical guide here. When one clings to approval, to the image others hold of us, to a future that looks safe, one invites the cage. When one loosens the grip; not by abandoning relationship, but by understanding that value is not contingent; a softer life becomes possible.

Detachment looks like this: a mother can love a child and still allow that child to make mistakes. A partner can care and yet accept that the loved one needs space to be themselves. A workplace can admire productivity without using it as a measure of human worth. Detachment is not withdrawal of love; it is the refusal to make love conditional on compliance. It frees both parties.

Practical exercises help: imagine holding a cup of water tightly; the longer you hold it, the more you notice strain. Loosen the grip and the body relaxes. Practice imagining outcomes and releasing them. Each time gratitude replaces demand, the inner knot loosens.

The Burden of Comparisons

Comparison is the hammer that forges cages. In families, comparisons work like a currency. "Your cousin got married at twenty-five." "Look at what we sacrificed for your brother." "Why can't you be more like her?" Each sentence creates metrics that are not the child's own. Children learn to perform to meet these metrics. They learn to hide failure, inflate success, and measure self-worth against someone else's curve.

There is also the hidden cycle: parents compare to preserve the family's image, believing that if the children measure up, their sacrifices are validated. The child grows, internalizes this economy, and can later become an adult who measures others by the same scale. The wound moves across generations, a baton of unmet needs and misunderstood love.

Consider a father who praises a neighbour's son for a promotion and then remarks with a sigh that his own daughter "chooses a fragile life of art." The daughter hears: "My choices are less legitimate." She begins apologizing for her passions. If she later succeeds, the family will often say, "We raised her well," and the credit will be framed as their victory. If she fails, the blame will be called proof that she lacked prudence. Either way, the child's agency is bought and sold.

The antidote is acceptance. When a child compares and later forgives the parent for their fear; recognizing it as limited sight not malice; a new lineage can start: one that values effort over image, curiosity over conformity. Parents, too, must be taught that their longing for social approval often costs the child's inner life more than the praise is worth.

The Forgiveness: The Unseen Libeartion

Forgiveness is not a sentimental act; it is the last stage of real power. To forgive is to disentangle one's life from the past's tight cords. One does not forgive because the other was right; one forgives because continuing to carry the hurt is a heavier price than letting it go.

There are three forms of forgiveness necessary here.

Forgiving others. This does not mean condoning behavior that hurt. It means recognizing the human limit of those who harmed you; that they acted from fear, scarcity, ignorance, or their own wounds. When she forgives a parent who compared her, she is not saying the comparisons were okay; she is saying she will no longer let those comparisons own her life.

Forgiving oneself. This is perhaps more radical. We often become prison guards of our own heart; repeating the sentence that we failed, that we should have tried harder, that we owe someone an apology. Self-forgiveness means seeing that choices were made with the information available then, with the courage available then. It is releasing the heavy ledger we carry.

Forgiving the story. The narrative one spins; "I am the failed daughter," "I am the rejected lover," "I always give more"; binds identity to an incident. To forgive the story is to tell a new one: "I learned," "I am learning," "I will choose differently."

Forgiveness is practical. It takes the mind off re-rehearsing the wound and gives it back to the present. It is the bridge that takes energy from complaint to action.

The Return to Oneness (*Anekantavāda*)

One of the great liberating insights is that truth is many-sided. The doctrine of *Anekantavāda* teaches that every perspective holds a fragment of truth. When argued with single-mindedness, life feels like a duel. When one embraces plurality, conflict softens.

Imagine two people arguing: one says, "You never listen." The other says, "I do listen." Both are true in their partial view. One communicates pain; the other has a different impression. If listened to without claiming absolute dominance, a conversation becomes an exploration, not a battlefield.

This has implications for breaking the cage. When a mother criticizes, it may be fear dressed as advice. When a partner withdraws, it may be confusion dressed as indifference. When a friend offers solutions, it may be their way of helping. Recognizing plurality does not eliminate pain, but it reduces the tendency to make others the absolute cause of your suffering.

Practically, this becomes a habit: before concluding that "they are cruel," ask, *What might their fear be?* Before assuming "I am unlovable," ask, *What evidence contradicts this claim?* These questions expand the frame and loosen the cage's force.

The Choice That Heals

At the center of breaking the cage is a choice; not a dramatic edict, but a daily, small agreement with oneself. It is the moment one decides; again and again; to choose presence over pleasing, to choose truth over ease.

Practical steps:

- ***Start small.*** Choose one thing this week that is for you only. It can be a walk, a page of writing, a truth told at a small family dinner.
- ***Protect the inner hour.*** Dedicate thirty minutes a day to do nothing but listen to yourself. No phone, no agenda. Sense the body, the breath.
- ***Say one truthful sentence.*** Practice saying one sentence that is honest and kind: "I'm feeling

overwhelmed today." "I need help with this." "I want to try this."

- ***Say no, where "no" is real.*** Use a short, calm refusal. No drama. *No guilt-ordeal.* Practice makes it possible.
- ***Create a tiny ritual of return.*** Each night, list three moments when you chose yourself. This trains the mind to notice agency.

The choice to act is difficult because it risks the fracturing of relationships built on predictable roles. But the alternative is a slow corrosion: a life where the self is borrowed from what others approve of.

Repairing the Relationships

Breaking the cage is not only solitary work. Where possible, repair can and should be attempted. This is subtle work: it asks for humility, clarity, and courage.

State your truth calmly. Instead of saying, "You always pressure me," try, "I feel pressured when decisions are made for me without my voice." This changes the frame.

Ask for one thing. Make a single request; not a list. "I would like one evening a week where I choose what we do." Small changes create trust without triggering the old dynamics.

Offer to see their fear. "I understand you worry. Can I share how that worry affects me?" This invites empathy without defensiveness.

Repair does not guarantee reconciliation. Some relationships will never change. That truth is hard but liberating: it clears energy for those that can evolve.

Living with the Paradox: Loving and Letting Be

Perhaps the deepest teaching is to love fully while letting go of the compulsion to control outcomes. You can care and also accept that others will choose differently. You can protect your boundaries while holding compassion for their limits.

A parent might never fully understand a child's choice. A partner may always prefer a version of you that is easier to hold. That is the human condition. You are not always the hero of another's story; and neither are they the villain of yours.

Practice: walk into a room and hold the intention, *I will do my part with honesty and then let the rest be.* The tension of needing to fix everything will ease.

The Small Practices That Become a Life

Credit should be given to the daily acts; the small practices that unglamourously rebuild a person.

- ***Morning Attention***: five minutes of breath and intention. Not prayer, but orientation. "Today I will notice one decision that is mine."
- ***Evening Inventory***: three lines of reflection. What was chosen for self? What yielded to fear? No judgment; only record.

- ***The Gentle Boundary***: practice a polite, firm refusal. "I can't help tonight." "I will arrive at 8, not 6."
- ***The One Honest Conversation***: once a week, speak for ten minutes about something that matters to you, uninterrupted.
- ***The Forgiveness Ritual***: write a letter you do not send. To parent, partner, friend, even yourself. Fold it and breathe. Keep it only to release energy.

These acts accumulate like small currencies paid toward freedom. Over months and years, they replace the old capital of approval with the new capital of integrity.

The Weight of Generational Love

One nuance must be offered gently: many who raise walls do so with scarcity born of their time. Parents who compare once had reasons; poverty, limited opportunity, survival strategies. Their demand for image and success often protected the family from external harm. When a child grows and feels wounded, they may later see the truth: parents gave what they had.

This recognition is not an excuse for harm but a context for compassion. The child who forgives after seeing the parent's frightened horizon begins to heal two ways: they release the blame, and they inherit, as a gift, a space to parent differently, should they ever choose.

The paradox is that the act of healing one's wound often frees the next generation. One forgiven comparison can reduce the chain's weight not just for you but for those you love.

The Quiet Courage of Returning

Courage looks different in this work. It is not always dramatic. Often it is the small bravery to sit with a friend's disappointment, to hold one's ground at a family photo, to buy oneself a ticket and sit alone in a train compartment with the right to be.

At the heart of courage is a discipline of attention. When the mind wanders to "they will be angry," bring it back: "What do I choose?" When the body tenses at the thought of saying no, breathe through it once more. Each small act of courage rewires the nervous system.

The reclaimed life is not one of certainty but of fidelity to one's inner compass. That is the new measure of success.

The Soul Is Born to Be Free

This is the hardest and the simplest sentence: souls are not meant to be perfected by others. Each soul arrives with a unique learning curve. Some learn compassion through loss, others through success. When a child compares their life to another's and later blames parents for limits, the child is both right and wrong. Right, because limitations were real. Wrong, because parents did their best within their horizon.

Reconciliation is to hold both: the injustice that shaped the childhood and the gratitude for survival. To hold these together is the practice of maturity. It allows the soul to remember that freedom is an inside job and that the lessons of the world are both harsh and necessary.

One does not negate pain by inventing excuses. One relieves pain by seeing the whole shape of it. The soul chooses to be alive, messy and glorious, to learn and to leave with a conscience that knows it tried.

The Choice to Leave a Different Legacy

Once unshackled, one acts differently. The parent who once measured a child's worth by achievement now learns to ask: *What makes you curious?* The partner who demanded compliance now listens for longing. The sibling who compared now celebrates the small rebellions.

Legacy is not wealth. It is the next field of possibility. By breaking one chain of expectation, you seed a different atmosphere. You craft a life that permits failure and praises trying. You show the people who watched you that love can ask less and hold more.

"Freedom is the small daily bravery of choosing yourself tenderly; the rest of the world will mend in time or it will not. Either way, you begin to breathe."

The Soul's Monologue

There will be a morning when the habit of self-betrayal will feel tired and old. On that morning, you will stand without hurry by a window and feel the weather as it is; rain, sun, a train passing; and you will not reflexively seek permission to be. You will breathe as if you are the keeper of a lamp. The lamp will tremble sometimes; the flame will sputter; winds will come and go. You will find, to your astonishment, that the flame answers not to who loves it, but to how gently it is tended.

Forgiveness will not come as a single dramatic act. It will be a thousand small courtesies you give yourself; the first cup of tea made with intent, the refusal that arrives without drama, the letter you write and fold under a stone until you are ready to read again. Your voice will not be loud at first. It will be patient, like a stream finding its path through rock. Some will cheer you on. Some will fear you. Some will not understand at all.

Let them have their fear. It does not unmake the quiet covenant you have signed with your own life: to try, to fall, to try again; not for applause but for the warmth of being who you are. There is no betrayal in choosing the path that teaches you what you needed to learn. There is only a return: to the self that was always waiting beneath the polite performance, beneath the small habitual apologies. The child in you will be surprised to hear a different tone and will laugh the way children laugh in the sudden sun.

Walk on. Walk with the small practices in your pockets as if they were stones of memory. When the world asks you to shrink, remember the line you made in your own heart that says, I will not. I will live fully, with tenderness and honesty. The cage will rattle. Some parts of your life will change beyond repair. Others will remain, softened.

In the end, it is not the iron of the cage that matters, nor the weight of the judgments, but the quiet decision to remember who you are. You do not owe your life to the maintenance of others' comfort. You owe it to the slow, unstoppable task of being yourself.

Go on. The world is what it is. You are what you choose. The sky is wide.

Chapter 7
To Love Self, To Live Again

The ultimate freedom begins with the self. To live fully, one must learn to honor, forgive, and cherish the inner voice; the quiet pulse that has always guided the soul. Loving oneself is not selfish; it is survival, healing, and the first step toward truly connecting with the world.

The Unheard Conversations

"The first morning I chose myself, even in small ways, the world didn't crumble; but I began to feel alive."

– 30-year-old, healing journey

"Loving myself wasn't arrogance; it was recognition that my soul deserves space to breathe, to make mistakes, to exist fully."

– 28-year-old

"I learned that living for myself did not hurt those I loved; it allowed me to return to them with a whole heart."

– 32-year-old

"I held my own hand for the first time,
Not as a child seeking comfort,
Not as a lover seeking assurance,
But as a friend who had waited decades to be seen.
The world outside continued its noise and haste,
Yet inside, I breathed with my own rhythm,
And in that breath, the chains loosened,
The cage fell silent,
And I finally remembered how to live."

The Moment of Choice

The path to self-love begins with a moment; sometimes quiet, sometimes terrifying; when a person says, *enough.*

It might be the realization that constantly bending for others has left the soul hollow. Or a single failure that reveals, painfully, that trying to please everyone costs more than it gives. In that moment, clarity begins. You understand: no one else can walk inside your shoes. No one else can heal your heart from the inside.

It is not rebellion. It is acknowledgment. *I have been surviving, now I will live.*

A young woman pauses in a park, watching children run free, and realizes she has spent decades trying to "fit in" everywhere. For the first time, she wonders: what would I do if I only answered to myself? The question is small, yet seismic. The first ripple of self-love begins here.

Listening to the Inner Voice

Most of life is spent tuning into the needs, desires, and opinions of others. To love oneself, one must first turn the dial inward.

- ***Notice the feelings.*** Anger, frustration, grief, excitement, joy; all are messages.
- ***Honor small preferences.*** A cup of tea, a quiet walk, a book chosen purely for oneself; these are declarations of self-respect.

- ***Say thoughts silently.*** Even if no one else listens, speaking internally validates the self.

It is a discipline of attention. Over time, the internal chatter becomes a conversation, not a battle. The once-muted voice of the soul grows stronger, clearer, and capable of guiding decisions without fear.

Releasing the Weight of Expectation

Self-love demands courage because it challenges invisible chains. Family expectations, societal norms, professional pressures; all have conditioned the mind to measure worth externally.

This section is not about neglecting responsibilities, but about *placing self-respect at the center of choices.*

A man resigns from a high-paying job he does not enjoy, not out of defiance, but out of honesty to himself. The world labels him reckless; he feels, for the first time in years, relief. The cage of others' expectations loosens, just enough to allow a breath of autonomy.

The release of expectation is quiet but profound. It is a recognition: *I will live my life; the world will continue.*

Embracing Imperfection

Self-love does not demand perfection. In fact, chasing perfection often cages the soul tighter than any external expectation.

Mistakes are reframed as lessons. Emotional reactions are seen as signals, not failures. Fear becomes a guide, not a jailer. The journey is iterative; each day offers new practice.

A woman practicing self-love allows herself to speak her mind in a meeting, even though she fears judgment. She stumbles over words. But the embarrassment is small compared to the satisfaction of truth. Step by step, the soul learns to move without armor.

Forgiveness as Liberation

To love oneself fully, one must forgive. Forgiveness is not optional; it is a bridge between old pain and new life.

- Forgive those who unintentionally caused harm.
- Forgive those who imposed limits, even with love.
- Forgive yourself for bending, hiding, or apologizing for decades.

This is radical freedom. One releases emotional debts and discovers that forgiveness is not about the other, but about reclaiming one's own energy.

Building a Personal Sanctuary

Self-love requires creating small spaces in life that belong entirely to oneself:

- Morning rituals: meditation, journaling, or simply being present.
- Boundaries: polite refusals, small acts of prioritization.

- Reflection: writing down victories, emotions, and moments of courage.

These are not indulgences; they are practices of survival and authenticity. Every small choice; to eat what you want, to speak your truth, to rest; is a brick in the foundation of self-trust.

The Ripple of Self-Respect

As self-love grows, it naturally radiates outward. Relationships begin to shift:

- Friends notice the quiet confidence and adjust their expectations.
- Partners recognize the independence and respond with authentic respect.
- Families gradually learn that love does not require compliance.

The world does not always change. But the individual within the cage changes first, and that alone alters every interaction.

Choosing Life Fully

Ultimately, self-love is a commitment *to* ***living fully***, without hiding, without apology.

It is waking up in the morning and choosing to see the day as a canvas, not a checklist. It is acknowledging fear, still walking forward. It is laughing, crying, and making mistakes; deliberately, freely, intentionally.

One realizes: life was never meant to be endured. It was meant to be felt, expressed, and lived.

"To love oneself is not vanity, but survival. To live fully is not luxury, but duty to the soul."

There will be mornings when the old fears return,
when the world still demands you shrink.
But you will remember the quiet promise you made:
to honor the pulse within.
You will let small joys bloom, let mistakes teach,
let love flow without strings.
You will walk your path with gentle courage,
carrying both gratitude and audacity.
The cage may whisper, but you will not listen.
The chains may rattle, but you will step forward.
You will live; not as others expect, not as the world demands,
but as your soul, finally, chooses.
And in that choosing, life itself will smile,
because the one it has been waiting for has finally arrived: you.

Part III
The Path Beyond the Cage
(Appendices & Healing Tools)

Rituals for the Soul

1. Dawn of Awareness; Morning Rituals

"Begin with yourself, before the world asks for your pieces."

Purpose: Connect with your inner self before the noise of the day.

Daily Practices:

- **Five minutes of silence:** Sit comfortably. Focus on your breath. Let thoughts pass like clouds.
- **Affirmations:** Speak gently to yourself:
  "I am enough. I honor my choices. Today, I walk my path."
- **Gratitude notes:** Write three things you notice or are thankful for; even a morning breeze counts.

Reflection Prompt:

- What small thing today am I grateful for that belongs only to me?

2. Whisper to the Soul

"The pen is a mirror of the heart; let it reflect without judgment."

Daily Practice:

- Capture emotions, small victories, and thoughts.
- Prompts:
  - *When did I honor my feelings today?*
  - *What did I do purely for myself?*

Weekly Reflection:

- Review your entries. Celebrate courage and honesty.

3. Gentle Boundaries; Protect Your Energy

"A boundary is not a wall; it is a declaration of self-respect."

Practice:

- Start small: say "no" to requests that drain you.
- Identify one area this week where you will honor your peace.

Reflection Prompt:

- What felt uncomfortable but necessary to protect myself?

4. Body as Home; Movement & Awareness

"The body remembers what the mind forgets."

Practice:

- Walk, stretch, or dance mindfully.
- Focus on sensations: "I feel my feet on the ground. I breathe. I am here."

Reflection Prompt:

- What did my body teach me today about presence or freedom?

5. The Pause; Mindful Response

"Pause before you act; hear yourself first."

Practice:

- Pause when frustration arises. Take three slow breaths.
- Ask: *"What is my truth right now? What do I need?"*

Visual Cue:

- Use a ring, bracelet, or touch your chest as a reminder to pause.

6. Small Kindnesses; Acts for the Self

"Kindness begins with the one who has been forgotten."

Daily Acts:

- Treat yourself gently: a warm tea, a favorite song, a quiet moment.
- Weekly: Write a letter to yourself celebrating your courage.

Reflection Prompt:

- How did I honor myself this week?

7. Expectation Detox; Release the Weight

"Others' hopes are not chains, unless you allow them to be."

Practice:

- Identify 2–3 choices made under pressure.
- Ask: *"What would I do if I answered only to myself?"*
- Start small; gradually reclaim decision-making power.

Reflection Prompt:

- Which choice felt most freeing today?

8. Nature & Stillness; Grounding

"Even stones witness without judgment; learn from their patience."

Practice:

- Spend 10–15 minutes outside, noticing textures, sounds, colors.
- Observe thoughts without engaging.

Reflection Prompt:

- How did the world outside mirror or contrast my inner world today?

9. Evening Closure; Release & Reflect

"Let the day go. Let the soul rest."

Practice:

- Note one lesson learned.
- Acknowledge one act of courage.
- Affirm: *"I did my best today. I honor myself. Tomorrow is mine."*

10. Weekly Soul Check-In

"The mirror of reflection shows not faults, but steps toward freedom."

Practice:

- Ask yourself:
    - *Did I live authentically this week?*
    - *Where did I bend unnecessarily?*
    - *What victories can I celebrate?*
- Adjust daily practices based on insights.

Reflection Prompt:

- One breakthrough this week:
- One area to practice more self-love:

"Each choice to honor yourself lays another stone in the path of freedom. The cage may murmur, the world may insist, yet your soul remembers: it was born to breathe fully, to feel deeply, and to live boldly; untethered, unbroken, and unapologetically alive."

Affirmation Chart

Purpose: To start the day by aligning mind, body, and soul, cultivating self-love, awareness, and emotional resilience. Reciting this daily creates a subtle but deep transformation.

Step	Focus	Affirmation / Script	Time
1	Grounding	"I am rooted, I am safe, I am present."	1 min
2	Self-Recognition	"I honor my thoughts, my feelings, my existence. I am worthy of love and care."	1 min
3	Release Burdens	"I release what is not mine to carry. I free myself from the weight of others' expectations."	1 min
4	Inner Strength	"I am capable. I am resilient. I am guided by my own wisdom."	1 min
5	Gratitude & Forgiveness	"I am grateful for this life. I forgive myself and others for all imperfections. My heart is open."	1 min
6	Daily Intention	"Today, I will act with awareness. I will honor my needs. I will speak my truth. I will notice joy and small blessings."	1–2 min

7	Visualization	"I walk my path with love for myself. I am the keeper of my soul. Today, I live fully."	1 min

Credit: *Inspired by Bhavna Yog of* ***Shri Praman Sagar Ji Maharaj****, a practice that has positively impacted millions worldwide.*

Appendix

Author's Note to the Appendix

When I began writing this book, and walked further on this path, I realized something profound; pain is never singular. It travels quietly from one heart to another, wearing different faces but carrying the same weight.

The emotions you have read in these pages are not just fragments of one life. They echo in hundreds of voices I have had the honor to hear; voices that were trembling, fierce, soft, broken, and brave all at once.

This appendix is a humble attempt to honor those voices. These are not numbers on a survey sheet. These are *real lives*, *unspoken struggles*, *unanswered questions*, and *delayed liberations*. Each interaction added a brick to the foundation of this book, making it more than a reflection of one person's pain; it became a mirror held up to society.

If this book finds its way to your heart, it is because it carries many hearts within it.
May these collective experiences remind you:

- You are not the only one.
- Your emotions are not weakness.
- And even in silence, there is a language that binds us together.

Why This Survey Matters?

This book is more than my words; it carries the quiet echoes of those who have walked through the storm. Over the course of structured and unstructured conversations with over 100 individuals; students, professionals, homemakers, parents, partners; a mosaic of pain, resilience, and unspoken battles began to form.

This appendix is dedicated to those real voices.

Some shared their fears through silence, some through trembling hands, and some with a courage they did not know they possessed. What unites them is a single thread: a yearning to be seen, understood, and to reclaim their own reflection from the world's distorted mirrors.

Survey Methodology: Listening to the Silence

1. Purpose of the Survey

The survey was designed not as a rigid research experiment but as a **sensitive, human-centred inquiry**; a way to listen deeply to people who often remain unseen behind smiling faces and practiced "I'm fine" sentences.

The goal was simple yet profound:

- To understand how emotional cages are formed through personal, familial, and societal expectations.
- To explore how individuals experience and express their inner struggles; depression, guilt, frustration, self-doubt.
- To identify the invisible barriers that prevent people from choosing themselves.
- And most importantly, to **honour their voices without judgment**.

This is not just data. This is *lived reality*.

2. Participant Profile

Over **100 individuals** between the ages of *18 and 60 years* were engaged over a span of *10 months*. They represented a diverse cross-section of society, ensuring a wide spectrum of perspectives.

Category	*No. of Participants*	*Key Demographics*
College Students	30	Age 18–25, urban/semi-urban
Working Professionals	35	Age 25–40, mixed sectors
Homemakers	15	Age 30–55
Senior Citizens	10	Age 50+
Others (Freelancers, Entrepreneurs, Artists, etc.)	15	Age 20–60

Inclusion Criteria:

- Individuals who expressed or hinted at emotional struggles.
- Willingness to share lived experiences voluntarily.
- Participants from different socio-economic and educational backgrounds.

This approach allowed both *breadth* (diverse life stages) and *depth* (emotional complexity).

3. Data Collection Method

The methodology blended structured and unstructured techniques to preserve both consistency and emotional honesty.

a) In-Depth Conversations

- Conducted mostly in person or through secure voice/video calls.
- Duration: 30 to 90 minutes.
- Focus: creating emotional safety rather than extracting information.
- Some participants chose to write their experiences after the conversation.

Being worked as a career counsellor, it was easy for the students and youths to open with me with their struggles as they have already heard me in seminars and public events. Many participants opened only after moments of silence, showing that the richest data often lies between words.

b) Observation of Non-Verbal Communication

- Silence, tears, hesitation, repeated phrases, changes in tone and breathing; all carefully noted.
- These observations often carried the real emotion more powerfully than language.

4. Ethical Considerations

The survey respected dignity and emotional safety above everything else.

- **Confidentiality:** No real names or identifying details have been used in this book. Composite characters and fictionalized scenarios were created to protect privacy while preserving the emotional truth.
- **Consent:** Every participant was clearly informed that their stories may contribute to a published

work. Participation was voluntary, and withdrawal was allowed at any point.

- **Non-interference:** This was a space of listening, not therapy. No participant was pressured to share what they did not wish to.

This ethical clarity helped build deep trust, resulting in more authentic narratives.

5. Structure of the Interaction

Each conversation followed a gentle flow rather than a rigid questionnaire:

1. **Opening Warmth** - Creating a safe emotional space.
    - "Tell me about your day... not the one you show the world, the real one."
    - Light conversation, no pressure to disclose.
2. **Guided Exploration** - Inviting deeper reflection.
    - "What's the one thought that visits you the most these days?"
    - "When did you last feel completely seen?"
3. **Anchoring Questions** - Tracing roots of pain and expectation.
    - "Whose voice do you carry in your head the loudest?"
    - "If the world wasn't watching, what would you do differently?"
4. **Silent Acknowledgment** - Allowing silence to speak.

- No forced answers, no corrections, no advice.

5. **Closing Grounding** - Restoring emotional balance before goodbye.
   - "You have shared something powerful today. Thank you."

This organic structure mirrored how pain actually unfolds in real life; not as straight answers, but as layered emotions.

6. Key Emerging Patterns

From over a hundred narratives, five recurring emotional patterns emerged:

1. **Invisible Expectations**; Most people did not realize how heavily others' expectations shaped their identity.
2. **Muted Voices**; A deep longing to be understood without being judged.
3. **Self-Blame Loop**; When understanding does not come, frustration turns inward.
4. **Silent Revolutions**; Almost everyone described quiet acts of inner resistance they never spoke about.
5. **Delayed Liberation**; Many said, *"If I had understood myself earlier, I would have lived differently."*

These themes became the emotional skeleton on which this book rests.

7. Integrating Jain Philosophy

A unique layer of this survey was spiritual framing through pluralism; inspired by *Anekantvada*, the Jain philosophy that teaches no single perspective holds the entire truth.

During conversations, instead of debating right or wrong, participants were gently reminded:

- "Your parents' truth and your truth can coexist."
- "What hurts you may not be visible to them; and vice versa."
- "Freedom isn't always about changing people; sometimes it's about understanding their angle without losing yours."

This approach defused blame and allowed participants to see their cages not only as prisons; but also, as places they have the power to walk out of.

This methodology is not here for academic weight alone. It exists to show *you are not alone.*

Every story you have read in this book echoes a real heartbeat somewhere.
Each concept, each stanza, each tear has a face behind it.

When you hold this book, you are holding their silence, their courage, their small yet defiant steps toward light.
And perhaps, your story will become someone else's quiet permission to breathe again.

Survey Themes & Sample Questions

A. Identity and Expectations

- When you close your eyes, who are you without roles or titles?
- Whose voice do you hear most often in your mind? Is it yours?
- How much of your life today is a choice and how much is a compromise?

B. Emotional Landscape

- How often do you feel truly understood?
- What emotion visits you the most – anger, fear, guilt, numbness, or something unnamed?
- When was the last time you felt safe just being yourself?

C. Family, Society, and Invisible Rules

- What is the most repeated sentence you have heard from your family?
- If you could say one thing without fear, what would it be?
- How has society's idea of 'success' shaped your life decisions?

D. Depression & Mental Struggle

- How does your pain usually express itself; silence, withdrawal, over-performance, or conflict?
- What do you wish someone had told you at your lowest point?
- What is one thing you have been hiding behind the sentence "I'm fine"?

E. Healing & Liberation

- What would change in your life if you stopped waiting for others to understand you?
- When you imagine healing, what does it look or feel like?
- What is one promise you want to make to yourself today?

Affirmation & Bhavna Yog Practice

(Inspired by the teachings of Shri Praman Sagar Ji Maharaj)
This practice is not a chant of denial but a gentle reminder to return to oneself. Recite these lines **every morning** with closed eyes, soft breathing, and awareness of your heartbeat.

Daily Self-Affirmation Script

"Today, I choose to return to myself.

I am not my mistakes, nor anyone's expectations.

I was born free; my worth is not on trial.

I bless those who could not see me, for they too carry unseen weights.

I forgive the world for being blind, and myself for dimming my own light.
I walk in my shoes, and only I can feel the stones beneath.
I choose love. I choose peace. I choose me."
(Repeat slowly three times. Let every word be felt, not forced.)

Quotes & Reflections to Return To

These lines are drawn from the survey, ancient philosophies, and lived experiences. They are meant to be revisited in moments of doubt.

- "Your silence does not make you weak. It only means your heart speaks in a language the world forgot to learn."
- "The mirror is not broken. You were just looking into someone else's reflection."
- "Every goodbye to old expectations is an invitation to your real life."
- "You are not late. Your healing is arriving in its own season."
- "Forgiveness is not surrender; it's unlocking your own cage."

7. Creating Your Own Liberation Plan

This final section helps the reader translate reflection into *conscious action*; a bridge between the book and real life.

- **Step 1: Identify the Cage**
  Write down 3 expectations, voices, or fears that control your decisions.

- **Step 2: Reclaim Your Voice**
  For each expectation, write what *your* heart truly wants, without filters.
- **Step 3: Forgive & Release**
  Say aloud: "I understand why they expected this of me. I release it."
- **Step 4: Anchor Your Own Dream**
  Make one small actionable promise to yourself this week. It could be as simple as walking alone for 10 minutes; what matters is *agency*.
- **Step 5: Return Daily**
  Healing is not a single event. It is a ritual.

8. A Soul Unbound

"And one day, you will wake up and breathe without permission.
The mirror will not scare you, nor will their voices define your reflection.
The world will remain as it is – noisy, restless, imperfect.
But inside, a still river will flow.
A river that whispers, 'I have come home.'"

"No one can walk your path for you.
But the universe will hold your hand while you learn to walk with yourself."

In the noise of expectations, it becomes easy to forget our own voice.
This journal is not a test. There are no right answers, no timelines, no judgments.

This journal is designed to be a daily practice of awakening, not a discipline.
Each day has a prompt, a gentle affirmation, and space for reflection.
There is no pressure to be poetic or perfect.
Only honesty. Only softness.
It is a sacred space; between your heart and your pen.

You may write one line or a whole page. You may cry between sentences. You may pause and come back later. That *is the practice*. Healing does not happen in leaps; it happens in whispers.

"When you learn to sit with yourself, you no longer beg to be understood. You simply begin to understand yourself."

How to Practice

- Sit in silence for 3–5 minutes before writing.
- Place your hand on your heart, breathe slowly, and acknowledge your presence.
- Read the day's affirmation aloud like a prayer to your own soul.
- Write freely. Let the ink be the voice you could not speak.

Week 1 — Meeting the Self (Awareness)

| 1 | "What emotion has been living inside me, unspoken?" | "I give myself permission to feel everything without fear." |

____

____

____

____

____

| 2 | "If my soul could speak without interruption, what would it say today?" | "My voice matters, even when it trembles." |

____

____

____

____

____

| 3 | "What parts of me are tired of pretending?" | "I allow myself to be real – not perfect." |

____

____

____

____

____

| 4 | "What does safety feel like in my body?" | "I am learning to listen to the quiet language of my heart." |

| 5 | "Where do I feel unseen, and why does it matter?" | "I deserve to be witnessed – even by myself." |

| 6 | "Who am I when no one is watching?" | "My worth exists without performance." |

| 7 | "What do I need to forgive myself for?" | "I release the weight of self-blame and choose gentleness."

____

____

____

____

____

Open your heart for this week...

The First Crack

"Some wounds do not bleed.
They sit quietly in the bones,
waiting for someone; maybe you;
to name them.
And when you finally whisper their truth,
the silence does not break...
it softens."

Week 2 — The Unraveling (Letting Go)

| 8 | "What masks have I worn to be loved?" | "I am lovable even when I remove the mask." |

____

____

____

____

____

| 9 | "Whose expectations have shaped my silence?" | "I honor my truth over borrowed dreams." |

____

____

____

____

____

| 10 | "What would I do if I stopped asking for permission to exist?" | "My path is mine to walk – unapologetically." |

____

____

____

____

____

| 11 | "What pain have I carried that was never mine to hold?" | "I release what no longer belongs to me." |

____

____

____

____

____

| 12 | "Which memory still holds my heart hostage?" | "I choose to unchain myself from the past." |

____

____

____

____

____

| 13 | "What story about myself needs rewriting?" | "I am not my scars – I am the courage beneath them." |

____

____

____

____

____

| 14 | “What or who must I forgive, not for them but for my peace?” | “Forgiveness is how I return to myself.”

____

____

____

____

____

Open your heart for this week...

The Hollow Nights

"You will learn that letting go is not weakness.
It is your soul's way of returning home.
There will be nights when your chest feels hollow,
but remember;
hollow spaces are where light learns to rest."

Week 3 — The Quiet Rising (Reclaiming Power)

| 15 | "What boundaries do I need to create to breathe again?" | "Every 'no' I speak is a 'yes' to myself." |

____

____

____

____

____

| 16 | "Where do I shrink to keep others comfortable?" | "I allow myself to expand, even if others do not understand." |

____

____

____

____

____

| 17 | "What does self-respect look like for me?" | "I honor my own dignity with softness and strength." |

____

____

____

____

____

| 18 | "What brings light into my day – even a small flicker?" | "Tiny joys are sacred; I allow them in." |

| 19 | "If I trusted myself fully, what decision would I make today?" | "I am learning to trust the voice within." |

| 20 | "Where do I still seek validation I can give myself?" | "I choose to be my own mirror." |

| 21 | "What would loving myself look like in action?" | "Love begins with how I treat my own soul."

____

____

____

____

____

Open your heart for this week...

The Whisper

"They told you healing was loud;
a battle cry, a roar.
But healing is a whisper,
a trembling breath
that still chooses to stay.
Courage is not the absence of fear,
it is the warmth of your own hand
when the world turns cold."

Week 4 — Living Unbound (Becoming)

| 22 | "What dream have I silenced out of fear?" | "I give myself permission to want." |

____

____

____

____

____

| 23 | "What kind of life feels truly mine – not borrowed, not expected?" | "I have the right to design my own world." |

____

____

____

____

____

| 24 | "Whose voice do I need to turn down to hear mine clearly?" | "I choose clarity over noise." |

____

____

____

____

____

| 25 | "What does freedom mean to me – in words, in feeling?" | "I was born to move, to feel, to live." |

| 26 | "What part of me am I finally ready to embrace?" | "I welcome all of me home." |

| 27 | "Who am I becoming beneath the healing?" | "I am not broken – I am becoming." |

| 28 | "What will I no longer apologize for?" | "I owe the world my truth, not my compliance." |

____

____

____

____

____

| 29 | "What legacy of love do I want to leave in this world?" | "My presence itself is a quiet revolution." |

____

____

____

____

____

| 30 | "What would it mean to truly love myself – fiercely, tenderly, freely?" | "I am my own home. I am my own liberation." |

____

____

____

____

____

Open you heart for this week...

The Becoming

"One day,
your reflection will not ask for permission to smile.
The tears will still come,
but they will no longer feel like surrender.
They will feel like rivers finally finding the sea.
You will not need to be understood.
You will simply be;
and that will be enough."

The Tear & The Touch

Inspired by Bhavna Yog

- *Sit in silence.*
- *Place your hand on your heart.*
- *Let a single tear fall; no shame, no resistance.*
- *Whisper to yourself:*

"This pain is real.
This love is real.
And I am still here."

- *Touch your heart with the warmth of your palm.*

"No one can save me... but me.
And that is enough."

You won by yourself, for yourself

"I have walked through fire without leaving my own hand.
I have been misunderstood and still chosen love.
I have cried rivers, but they have not drowned me.
They have carved me.
I am not my darkness.
I am the sky that holds it.
I was born to live - not just survive."

I write not just to be heard, but to remind every heart that healing is possible, and freedom is a birthright.